THE PROS AND CONS OF LIVING OFFGRID

Table of Contents

1

WHAT IS "LIVING OFF THE GRID"?

Living off-grid does not mean living without electricity, nor does it have to mean a very rustic lifestyle. Simply put, being "off-the-grid" just means you are your own power company. You can be off-grid in the middle of nowhere, or you can be off-grid in the middle of everything.

Around the same time each month, millions of Americans go to their mailboxes seeking the comforts of a handwritten letter or their favorite magazine only to be greeted by white envelopes with miniature cellophane windows. We're all familiar with these mailers -- power, water, gas

2

and telephone bills, all conspiring to take your hard-earned money. For most people, paying utility bills is a tiresome and frustrating task. What if there was a way to get out from under the thumb of public utilities and produce your own sustainable energy? Well, there is. Going "off-grid" is becoming an increasingly popular choice for people looking to reduce their carbon footprint, assert their independence and avoid reliance on fossil fuels.

"The grid" is a common name for the power grid -- the linked system that delivers electricity to the masses. A typical house is connected to power, natural gas, water and telephone lines. Going off the grid means shunning these public utilities in favor of creating your

3

own energy. Some homeowners choose to be partially off the grid by supplying their own electricity and ditching their phone line, while relying on the convenience of city water and sewage. Others choose to live completely off-grid by digging wells or using a cistern system to collect water. A septic tank takes care of the sewage and, just like that, no more water bill either.

Why go off-grid?

There are many reasons to be off-the-grid, but typically off-grid (stand alone) solar electric systems are used in remote locations where connecting to the local utility grid is impossible or prohibitively expensive, in areas where grid power is inconsistent, or due to the appeal of an independent lifestyle. With an off-the-grid system, solar panels, a small wind

4

turbine, a micro-hydro system, or a combination of these technologies and others, is used to supply all of the power a cabin, home or business needs. In some off-grid systems a home backup generator may also be included, to supply power when the renewable technologies can't produce enough to meet demand.

Off-grid living completely relieves you of dependency on the electrical utility, because the system provides all of your power. Due to this, off-grid systems are generally larger than grid-ties. To be fully independent, a system must have a larger wind generator or array of solar panels, and greater battery storage capacity than in applications where grid power is available. However, if done properly,

5

living off-the-grid can save you thousands
of dollars over the life of the system.

6

ARE YOU CONSIDERING GOING OFF THE GRID?

Are you considering going off the grid completely? If so, here are some tips to keep in mind for maximum success.

For many, going 100% off the grid is a dream come true. Not only that it could save you money, but it also can bring you that incredible feeling of satisfaction, knowing that you are doing everything you can for the environment.

To reach that goal, however, you have to keep in mind that you cannot do it overnight. In fact it is a continuous process, and the best thing to do in order to ensure that you do not sacrifice your personal needs, is to do it all gradually and think everything through. You have to consider carefully the location of your

7

property, so that you can generate a maximum amount of renewable energy, and you will have to think of how to manage your water, drainage, and food supply, because yes, these are part of the "going off the grid" deal.

Living off the grid is one of the most romanticized parts of homesteading or simple living. It's often mistaken as a requirement for "true homesteading", whatever that means. While going off the grid is definitely not a challenge everyone can take on, it does have a lot of benefits for the dedicated family seeking authentic green living. Separating the myths from the realities about off grid living helps prevent anxiety and prepares you and

8

your family to decide if it's really right for you all.

9

THINGS YOU SHOULD CONSIDER BEFORE GOING OFF THE GRID

1. Realize what you are about to do.

Going completely off the grid means that you unplug from all the services that your home is connected to. These include not only the power grid, but also the water supply and community utilities, like garbage collection.

Having said that, nowadays there is nothing that can prevent you from having a comfortable yet sustainable and 100% off the grid lifestyle. Here is what modern technology has to offer:

Renewable energy is there for you- solar, wind and/or hydro power, even DIY

10

biogas plants– everything is within your reach.

The market offers large, light and super easy to install water storage tanks.

Compost toilets and compost bins are much more trouble.

Satellite and wireless technology is always there to keep you connected with the world.

Tips on insulation and home designs for heating and cooling are available to you from everywhere.

2. The most important things to know in advance:

Summer is hot

Winter is cold

Nights are dark

Gardens need good soil

11

Water does not run uphill

Find a way to handle these and you will be just fine.

3. Know how to stay warm.

This is the most important and challenging point of all, because solar panels alone can hardly ever handle the whole burden. Here are a few extra tips:

Fit a slow-combustion wood fire in the main living area

Insulate all walls and ceiling

Make use of passive heating, such as placing large glass doors in kitchen to face positive sun direction

Consider the suitable home interior and exterior design, including window size, placement, and coverings.

12

Do not allow large trees in the garden to block the incoming sun.

4. What is 'junk' really?

Going off the grid makes you realize how many things around you are completely unnecessary, and the other way round- things that you thought are junk are in fact extremely useful. Take a good look at all these things that eat up energy, waste water, or simply block the incoming light- you will be amazed.

5. The sun is your new best friend.

And this is not only because it hits your solar panels or helps you heat up the house in winter. The most important solar-powered item you will need to put your hands on will be the solar water heater. Incoming solar light warms up the water in your existing water tanks without additional power usage, allowing you to have a nice hot shower even in the coldest winters.

6. Reduce, Reuse, Recycle.

Going off the grid gives recycling a whole new meaning. As soon as you have something tat you want to dispose of, the first thing that crosses your mind is not whether it goes in the green bin, or the orange one. In fact, you ask yourself- "how else can I use it".

14

Bio-waste goes in the compost bin, jars become glasses or flower pots, plastic bottles make a greenhouse, cans make a room heather– just allow your imagination to go crazy.

7. Choose your location carefully.

This is very essential. The chosen location should have suitable soil and climate so that you can do essential gardening and grow your fresh produce. In addition, you will need plenty of sunshine, good amount of rainfall, and of course pleasurable landscape that you can enjoy.

Yes, unfortunately, going 100% off-grid somehow means that you will have to leave your old neighborhood behind and move to the country.

8. Get familiar with the off-grid currency and the community.

Off-grid currency is something that you do not think of before you have to actually use it. That is, in fact, everything, from the organic produce in your garden, all the way to your DIY skills, streetlights, cleaning abilities, cooking abilities, sewing abilities, etc., etc..

Get to know your neighbors and your community. The best advice and help could come from the most unexpected places.

16

BENEFITS OF GOING OFF THE GRID

A. Financial Independence

The idea of eliminating or at least reducing the monthly energy bills is the biggest attraction of off grid living for most homeowners and renters. Producing your own power and disconnecting from the power grid does free up hundreds of dollars in the monthly budget. This is especially true in energy intensive areas with cold winters and hot summers.

However, you're going to pay a lot of money upfront to achieve that reduction in monthly costs. If you're financing the investment in solar panels and other renewable energy equipment, you may pay nearly as much or the same as what

17

you currently spend per month on the equipment itself.

Many families find this is a worthwhile exchange since they still enjoy the other four benefits of going off grid while spending about the same. Do the math for yourself with this handy calculator based on your current energy usage, local energy costs, and renewable energy equipment costs to figure out your personal break even point for living off the grid.

B. Living Sustainably

For early adopters of solar voltaic panels and other home renewable energy systems, the benefit to the environment was well worth the high cost. Today's off the grid equipment is far less expensive,

18

but it's still one of the best ways to lower your carbon footprint. Generating your own power at home allows you to free yourself from the reliance on coal, natural gas, or other fuels that you don't agree with.

Green living doesn't require you to go completely off the grid anymore. Across the country there are dozens of expanding utility providers aiming to offer grid power that is generated partially or completely by renewable sources. Check into all of your sustainable living options before assuming you have to live completely off the grid just to reach your environmental goals.

C.Conscious Living Off the Grid

Other people who are experienced with living off the grid claim a deeper connection to their surroundings and loved ones after limiting the role of electricity in their lives. When you're trying to reduce stress with simple living, having a limited supply of power is definitely appealing.

No matter how many storage units and backup systems you install, you must remain conscious of your power usage at all times while off the grid. There's no constant and steady supply of power to keep pulling from endlessly. When you've drained all your batteries and the sun is down or hidden behind the clouds, you're either firing up a generator running on not-so-green fuels or going without power. Spending less time on electrical devices that serve as distractions can bring a family together as well.

D.Off Grid Power Resilience

Finally, the rugged individualist is usually after the concept of resilience and freedom that comes from living off the grid. Political changes won't cause your bills to rise or fall, and you won't have to worry about your utility company shutting down or charging you late fees. Natural disasters affect you much less. Just don't forget that you're the one who has to go out in the storm and clean up the debris to restore power, not the lineman hired by the utility company.

21

DISADVANTAGES OF GOING OFF THE GRID

But you can't forget the disadvantages of going off-grid either. You may have to move because a lot of places will not allow you to be completely off-the-grid, unless you are choosing to go solar, add a well, etc.

Also, if you have a family, you need to consider your children's well being in this process. Though going off-grid is appealing and the 'roughing it' method is obviously more cost-effective, a lot of states frown upon children living this type of lifestyle. You could easily be heading for legal trouble. So take all of your local laws into consideration before taking the off-grid plunge.

22

Plus, you must consider the investment you will be making into your property if you decide to go with the 'modern off-grid' option. It is not cheap, but you may very well deem the expense worth it.

Let's also not forget some of the lifestyle changes going off-grid might cause you to have to make. If you choose to go totally off-grid without any help from wind, solar, or hydropower your whole life will change. You will no longer be able to just run to the bathroom for a quick shower, or run water in your sink to wash dishes. You should really consider all of the lifestyle changes that will have to be made to adjust to this new off-grid lifestyle.

23

HOW TO LIVE OFF THE GRID

Off the grid. We use these words to describe everything from camping in the backcountry to traveling across cellular "dead zones" without service to removing ourselves from contemporary society in favor of a more in-tune relationship with nature. But, you may ask, what is "the grid." And how does someone live off of this seemingly elusive mechanism? Well, in short, it's all about self-sustainably in just about every aspect of the phrase. This includes shelter, power, food production, harnessing and recycling water, and managing waste without the assistance of outside influences. And while this may sound foreign in a contemporary communal age of convenience, it's not impossible.

Before we go into more details on how to live off the grid we need to establish a definition of what "the grid" actually means. In this instance, the grid in question here is referred to as the power grid – which is the linked system that delivers power (in the form of electricity) to the masses. Here, we have what is actually a fragile ecosystem of dependence that transfers energy generated on a mass scale from extra high voltage producers (such as coal, nuclear, or hydroelectric plants) through a distribution grid and into the homes or offices of consumers. Needless to say, just about every aspect of our daily lives is reliant on "the grid," so it's no secret that removing yourself from this system with the intentions of self-sufficiency is no easy task – the rewards, however, are quite fruitful. With that said, here's a brief guide on what you need to consider and how to get started.

26

1. SHELTER

It's no surprise you're going to need adequate shelter for such an expedition but odds are you're going to have to downsize a bit depending on your current home. Here, size matters and more space means great maintenance and power dependency. It's for these reasons we don't find any McMansions in the wild. Instead, off-the-grid individuals opt for small hand-built cabins, trailers,

27

or any number of tiny homes that are easily powered and maintained. Again, considering the amount of energy you need to sufficiently power your home without the assistance of government-run energy is key to successfully undertaking this task.

With this in mind, if building your own home isn't an option, there are a few options out there to get you started. Fortunately, an off-the-grid mentality isn't a new one these days so a handful of small brands work to cater to individuals looking for quick and easy ways to relinquish their dependency and start forging their own path. The Greenmoxie cabin, for instance, is one such example of an all-inclusive off-the-grid package that works to encompass all the

28

necessary elements of sustainable living with the exception of food production. There are also new flat-pack housing options as well that come equipped with solar panels and rainwater tanks that are portable and can be transported atop a trailer. These modules also allow families living in the backcountry to add more space to their homes when the time comes.

2. ENERGY

29

Possibly the key ingredient to living off-the-grid properly, energy in this instance has to be entirely self-sustainable. That means, most if not all the electricity utilized by you and your home needs to be generated onsite in one way or another. These days, the most popular means of accomplishing this is through harnessing the sun via solar panels and battery packs and fuel cells. Additional options include utilization of water and wind energy.

Whatever source you choose, you need to make sure the method is properly converting the raw energy into alternating current for your home. Solar panels, for instance, contain cells made up of silicon semiconductors that collect the suns energy and knocks electrons loose allowing them to flow freely. From here, the panel then forces these electrons to flow in one direction (creating a direct current) which is then covered into alternating current through an inverter. Wind energy works in a similar manner but in a more old world fashion in which propellers spin a shaft that in turn attaches to a generator via the hub of a rotor. The generator then converts this energy produced by the rotation into usable energy for your home.

Depending on where you decide to set up shop, you can power a home utilizing natural running water from rivers. Dubbed "micro-hydro energy" home-scale hydroelectric power is made possible by mechanical systems put in place that converts the force of flowing water in electricity for your home. Simply put, the flow from a river or stream is directed towards a wheel in a turbine that then converts the resulting rotational energy into usable electricity. Naturally, the amount of energy produced depends on both the volume of water and the angle through which it's flowing through the system. Because of such variables, these systems can produce anywhere between 75 to350-kilowatt hours a month and can get quite pricey at times. Therefore, caution should be exercised when installing these systems – since location and reliability of the water source should be strongly considered.

3. WATER

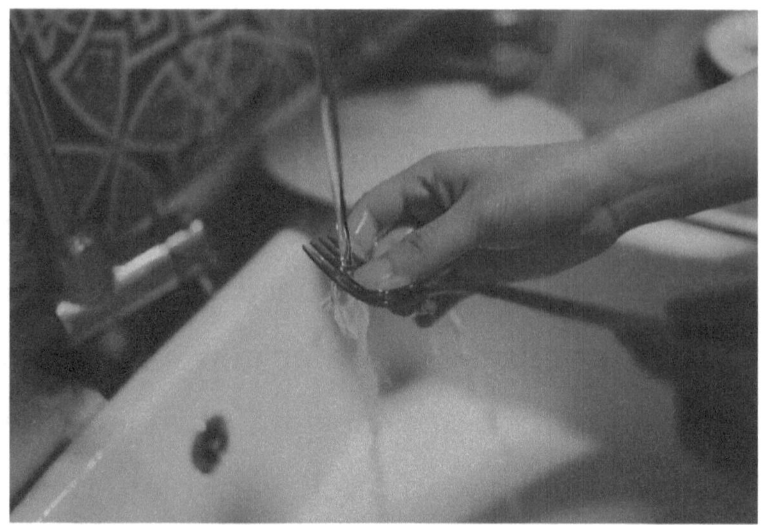

The next step in off-the-grid living is removing yourself from the ubiquitous city water lines. Surprisingly, unless you're opting to live in an arid desert, this is easier than you think. That's because water is practically everywhere. It falls from the sky, runs through rivers, streams, and lakes, and even beneath our feet as ground water. Therefore, tapping into these systems can be a great way to keep your produce alive and well (more on that later), your dishes clean and yourself washed.

The next step in off-the-grid living is removing yourself from the ubiquitous city water lines. Surprisingly, unless you're opting to live in an arid desert, this is easier than you think. That's because water is practically everywhere. It falls from the sky, runs through rivers, streams, and lakes, and even beneath our feet as ground water. Therefore, tapping into these systems can be a great way to keep your produce alive and well (more on that later), your dishes clean and yourself washed.

Catching rainfall through the use of a cistern is another way to keep the water flowing through your off-the-grid domicile. These tanks are commonly made out of concrete, steel or fiberglass and collect rainwater as it's collected via rain gutters on the roof of your home. If you opt to place the cistern on the top of your home, the weight of the water will allow easy access from inside, however, a pump will be needed if your tank is located below or at ground level. In addition, metal or clay roofing is the best option since they're much cleaner than shingled roofs.

4. LAND

Regarding land, some people say that the least amount of land you can get by with is ½ acre. Personally that seems rather small to me. I think 5 acres is more like it. You want to make sure the land is

35

habitable, that it can grow crops, that it's not in a flood zone and that it is relatively flat enough to put a house on and farm. As I mentioned previously having running water on your land is like having a gold mine, that is very important. You can find land for as little as $1,000 an acre and less but it probably wouldn't have water on it. I'm thinking it might cost about $5,000 to get a decent amount of land with some water on it but it's an educated guess from what I've researched. I recently did a little research on Craigslist and found a beautiful tract of land that was $123,000 for 160 acres of beautiful land. It was about one hour south of Portland, Oregon. If you went in with 16 people that would be approximately $7,500 for 10 acres of land in a great area! You could even divide it into 5 acres for less than $4,000. So you might have to look a bit but deals are out there and believe me the prices will continue to go down.

5. COMMUNICATION

Communication is also very important. Satellite Internet Services are one way to go and they are relatively inexpensive. Also ham radios are another source of off grid communication. I think communication is very important as you need to protect yourself and how can you do that if you don't know what is going on. The cost for this is about $300 start up and $60 a month. However, if no satellite service is available or if you just don't want the government knowing exactly where you are via your computer or cell phone you can always opt out and get a CB or ham radio and save the $60 bucks a month.

6. HEAT

In some areas of the country you might not have to worry about staying warm, but in others it will be a factor. If you build a cob house you will already be ahead of the game as they are very warm and it's easy to build a fireplace in them. In some states (like Ohio) you might be able to find a piece of land that has free natural gas on it, that would be a great boon as you wouldn't have to worry about finding and chopping wood. I think the most important factor regarding warmth is to make sure you build a house that keeps the warmth in in the first place. After that you can consider, wood-stoves or solar panels. I have just included this in the price of the house for a fireplace. However, if you do need a wood-stove, a really good one will cost you about $5,000. They have some at Lehman's hardware that are just wonderful and will heat your water as well. Personally, a wood-stove is on my must have list.

7. TRANSPORTATION

Personally, I would like to never own a car again as they require too much invasion of privacy. You have to get a license, register it, get insurance and on and on it goes. So my preferred method of transportation would be a tricycle. They have storage ability and are more stable

39

than bicycles. I know, I know it might be difficult to go without a vehicle because of what could come up but another method might be to actually have a couple of horses or even a donkey on your property. At least animals replenish themselves! A tricycle costs about $1,000 to $2,000 dollars. Another alternative is to make your own solar car (you can find them on You Tube), however to do this would cost about $5,000, you can also buy a diesel engine car and grow your own vegetable oil but again the cost would be up there at about $5,000.

8. PROTECTION

Protection: Well, there are several ways that you can protect yourself. The first thing that comes to mind are fire-arms

40

and I'm all for that but you'd better know how to clean them and use them before you get them. However, there are other methods to protect yourself as well. One method is by hiding. If you put a living roof on all your buildings it might be difficult for anyone flying over to notice that you are there. If your greenhouse or even your main house is partially underground it also would be difficult to know if you are there. Offense is just as important as defense. Dogs are also good sources of protection as are security cameras and security fences that are invisible. These costs will vary but should be minimal.

9. FOOD

Just like water, there is no life without food. So, ideally, you're going to want to find ways of growing and harvesting your own food around your newly established home. This can be accomplished through basic farming techniques in which you can grow perennial vegetables, even planting a few fruit trees in the process. And, depending on the size of your land, growing and harvesting wheat is also an ideal way to keep living expenses on the low end. Also, if you know how to hunt and dress wild game in addition to farming you can essentially live a hearty and fulfilling existence without the need to ever head into town for food. And for those looking to keep their dairy fixation alive and well. Adding a few goats and chickens into the mix couldn't hurt either.

However, if the "survivor man" approach isn't in your repertoire, it's suggested that you proceed with caution when purchasing products. We say this because without utilizing city waste disposal or sewer lines, garbage can pile up quite quickly. That's why when purchasing food items, recycling and composting are two things to strongly

43

consider – especially the latter if you plan on removing yourself entirely. Therefore, growing your own fruits and vegetables, and avoiding packaged foods will go a long way in keeping your carbon footprint to a minimum. It's also wise to pick up some literature on the subject. From guides on permaculture to field manuals on edible fruits and berries in the wild to field-dressing manuals on wild game, all options are highly advised as education shouldn't cease to be part of your daily routine when living out in the backcountry.

10.   WASTE

Finally, getting off the city's sewer line is the last step in ensuring your independence from public utilities. And unless you want things to get really miserable real quick, we advise in investing in the simplest and easiest way to manage the day's waste – a septic system. Basically, the right septic system will catch and release your waste water and slowly release it into a nearby drain

45

field through a series of perforated pipes. And since the soil acts as a natural biological filter, the harmful waste bacteria are then absorbed as nutrients by the soil.

There is one caveat, however, despite the seemingly simplified and sustainable nature of a septic system, they do require yearly service by a professional in the field. Now depending on how removed you are from civilization, you could install your own septic system with a little know-how, but these are illegal in most areas and could result in hefty fines so it's highly recommended to proceed with caution here. Another option, albeit a more old-world one, is to build an outhouse or privy. Here, privacy is granted thanks to the small structure and a basic vent system. One thing to consider when building an outhouse: you're going to want to make sure it's downhill -but above the flood plain – from your water sources. It's also useful to occasionally add lime or sawdust down the outhouse pit to help control odor and aid in decomposition.

Conclusively, it's worth noting that no amount of preparedness can make up for a mindset that's not in sync with this lifestyle. That is, overindulgence of first world conveniences is not a reality here. Expect to work harder and longer for seemingly simple pleasures like dinners, leaving the lights on, taking extended showers, or even washing dishes. Washing clothes by hand would also come highly recommended. Remember, your resources are fragile in this environment so it's important to treat your energy and water reserves as gingerly as possible. It's important to manage your energy use as well. Because while appliances and lighting will work with the help of solar and wind power, they may all not function properly at the same time. Therefore, it's important to live a more conservative lifestyle out here. All told, living off the grid at its core is a great way to reduce your carbon footprint on the world while gathering a deeper understanding of the world around us. The lifestyle offers peace and quiet in the wilderness while forcing you to live an examined and minimalist lifestyle. Sure, some of the pleasures of contemporary

48

urban life are gone, but so are the stresses that come with the modern day hustle. It's a small price to pay for the independence and fulfillment you'll feel when enjoying a meal you're caught, grown and prepared yourself inside a sustainable home lit from the previous day's sunlight before an evening shower compliments of your personal well. No utility bills, no junk mail, no crowds.

*Dedicated and inspired by the Steven Spacil move to British Columbia 2018.

www.ingramcontent.com/pod-product-compliance
Lightning Source LLC
Chambersburg PA
CBHW051358250726
48656CB00006B/2161